MANDACOLORIT CRAFT

Origami For Beginners

NEW WAYS TO CREATE ELABORATE MASTERPIECES WITH PAPER

TABLE OF CONTENTS

04 *Owl*	**09** *Parrot*	**12** *Pelican*
16 *Baby penguin*	**19** *Pigean*	**22** *Pigeon*
25 *Pigeon*	**29** *Swan*	**32** *Duck*
35 *Flying duck*	**39** *Ostrich*	**42** *Penguin*
46 *Owl*	**49** *Duck*	**53** *Sparrow*
	57 *Pigeon*	

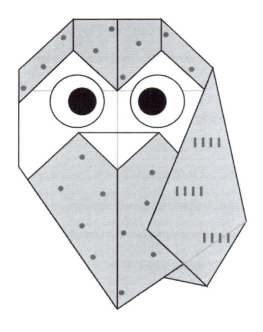

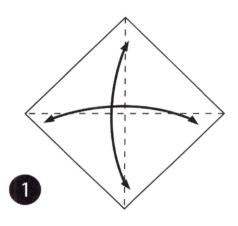

Step 1) Fold and unfold the paper in half both ways.

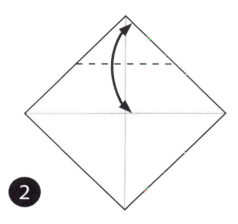

Step 2) Fold the paper down along the dotted line and then unfold it.

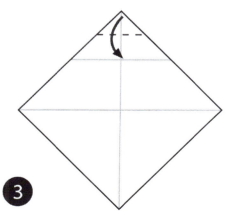

Step 3) Fold the paper down along the dotted line.

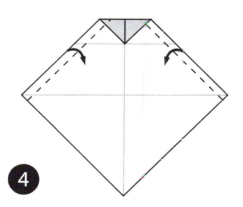

Step 4) Fold both sides in along the dotted lines.

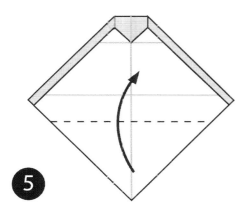

Step 5) Fold the paper up along the dotted line.

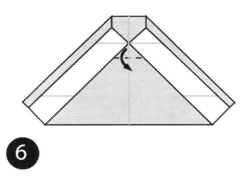

Step 6) Fold the top layer of paper down along the dotted line.

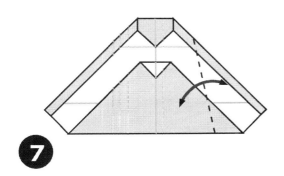

Step 7) Fold and unfold the paper along the dotted line.

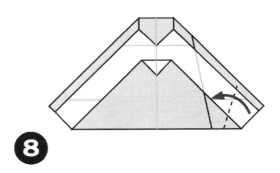

Step 8) Fold the paper in along the dotted line.

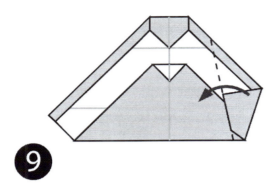

Step 9) Fold the paper in along the crease from earlier.

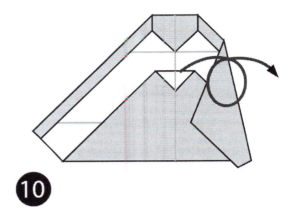

Step 10) Turn the paper over.

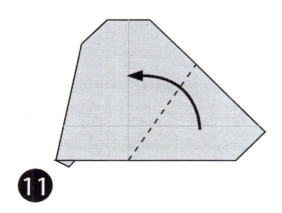

Step 11) Fold the paper along the dotted line.

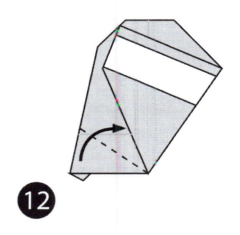

Step 12) Fold the paper in along the dotted line.

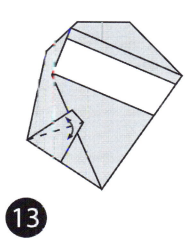

Step 13) Fold and unfold the paper along the dotted line.

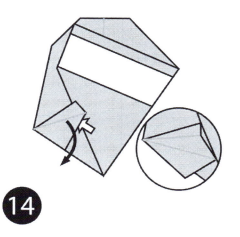

Step 14) Open the paper and Squash Fold it flat using the existing crease.

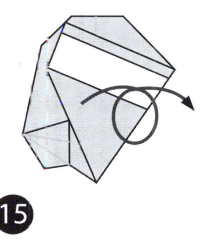

Step 15) Turn the paper over.

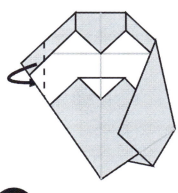

Step 16) Fold the paper behind the model along the dotted line.

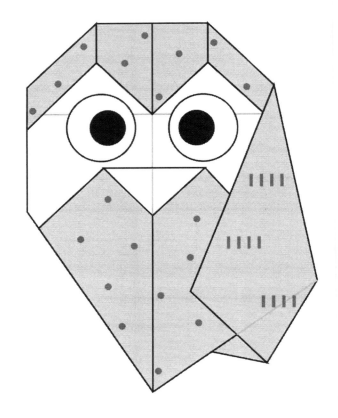

The complete owl

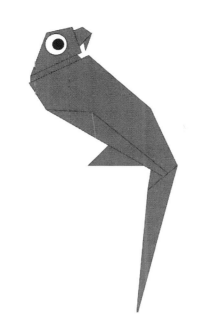

Parrot

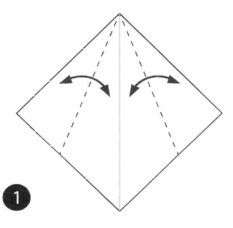

Step 1) Fold the paper in half and unfold it, then fold both sides in to the centre and then unfold them.

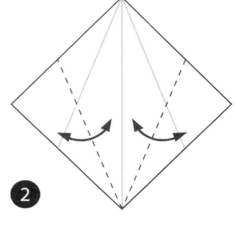

Step 2) Fold both sides in to the centre along the dotted lines.

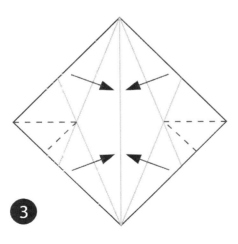

Step 3) Make a Rabbit Ear Fold on each side resulting in a Fish Base.

Step 4) Fold the flaps out along the dotted lines.

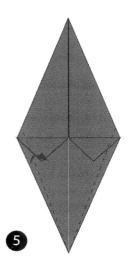

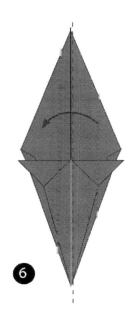

Step 5) Fold both sides in along the dotted lines.

Step 6) Fold the model in half.

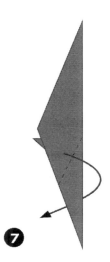

Step 7) Fold the paper behind along the dotted line.

Step 8) Make 3 folds along the 3 dotted lines.

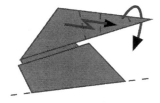

Step 9) Make a Pleat Fold and then one more fold at the tip of the beak.

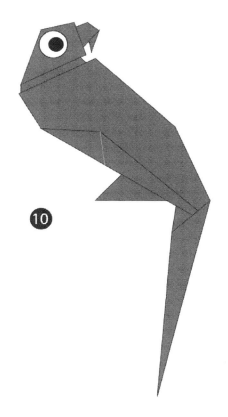

The complete parrot

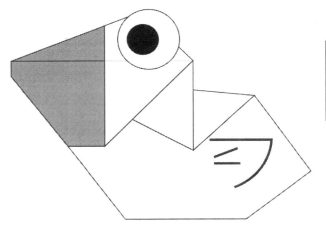

Pelican

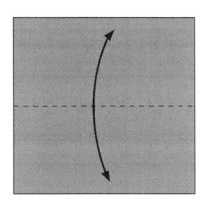

Step 1) Fold the paper in half and then unfold it.

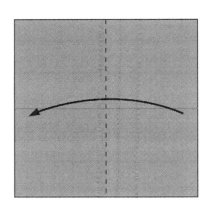

Step 2) Fold the paper in half the other way.

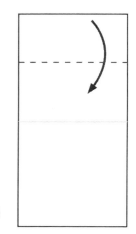

Step 3) Fold the top of the paper down along the dotted line.

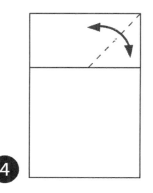

Step 4) Fold the paper along the dotted line and then unfold it.

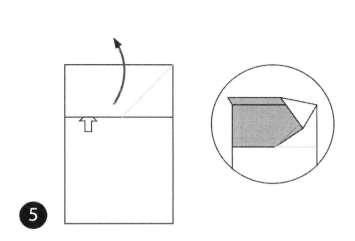

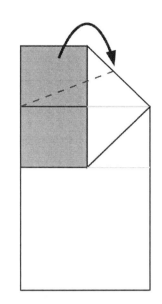

Step 5) Open up the top part of the paper and Squash Fold it flat using the existing creases.

Step 6) Fold the paper behind along the dotted line.

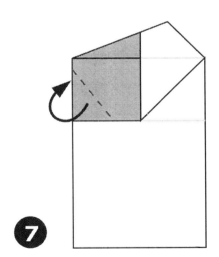

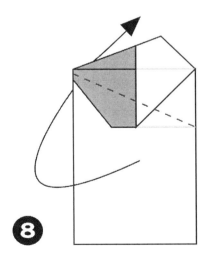

Step 7) Fold the paper underneath along the dotted line.

Step 8) Fold the paper up and behind along the dotted line.

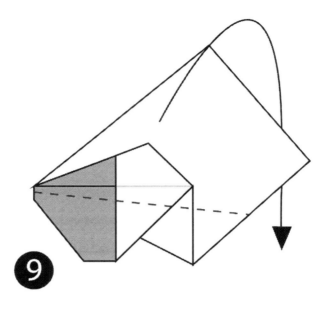

Step 9) Fold the paper down along the dotted line.

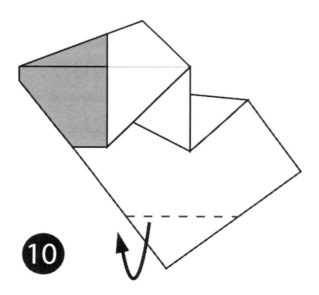

Step 10) Fold the paper underneath along the dotted line.

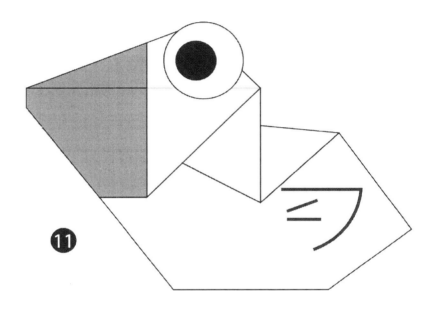

The complete pelican

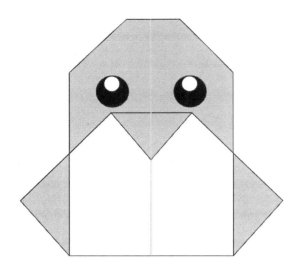

Baby penguin

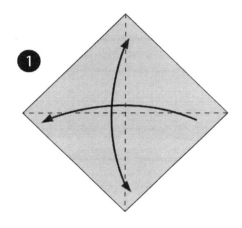

Step 1) Fold and unfold the paper in half both ways.

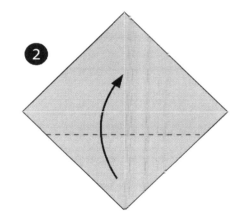

Step 2) Fold the paper up along the dotted line.

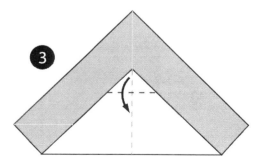

Step 3) Fold the tip of the top layer of paper down along the dotted line.

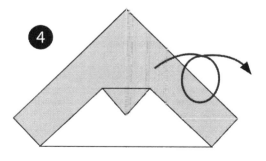

Step 4) Turn the paper over.

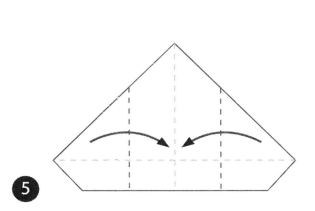

Step 5) Fold both sides in along the dotted lines. One side will be on top of the other.

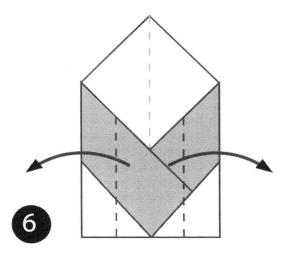

Step 6) Fold both sides back out along the dotted line.

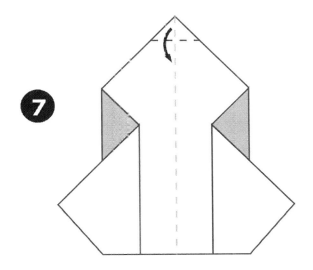

Step 7) Fold the top of the paper down along the dotted line.

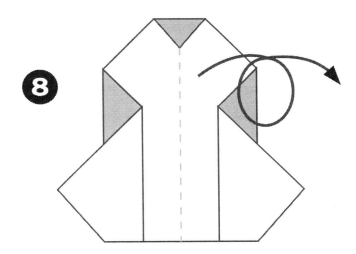

Step 8) Turn the paper over.

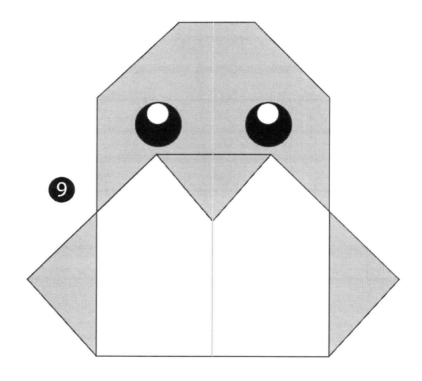

The complete baby penguin

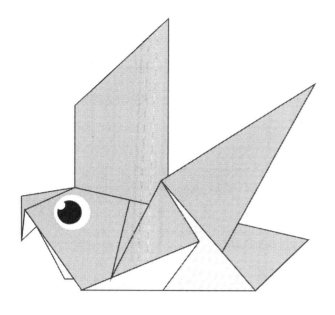

Pigeon

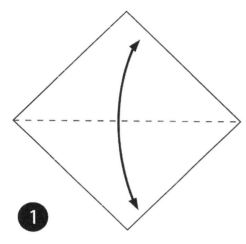

Step 1) Fold the paper in half and then unfold it.

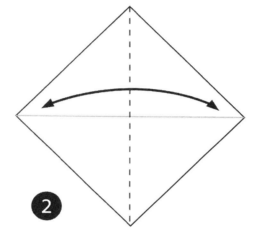

Step 2) Fold the paper in half the other way.

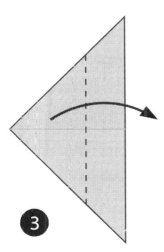

Step 3) Fold both layers of paper to the right along the dotted line.

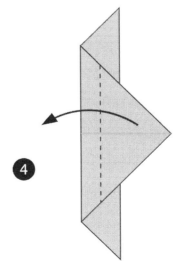

Step 4) Fold the top layer of paper to the left along the dotted line.

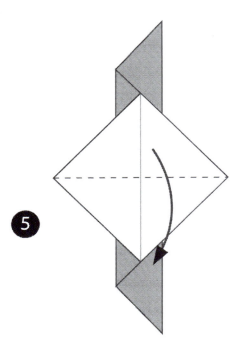

Step 5) Fold the model in half down along the dotted line.

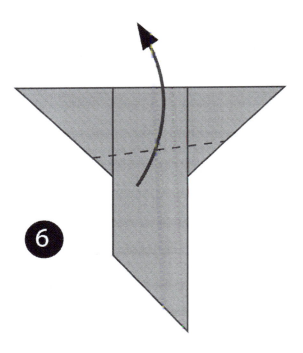

Step 6) Fold the top flap of paper up along the dotted line and then repeat on the other side.

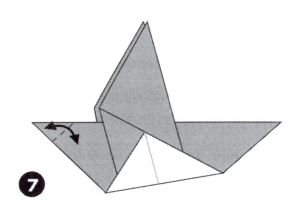

Step 7) Fold the paper along the dotted line and then unfold it.

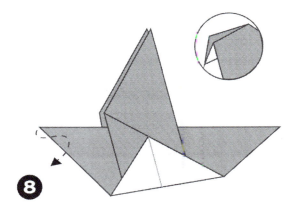

Step 8) Make an Inside Reverse Fold using the crease from the previous step.

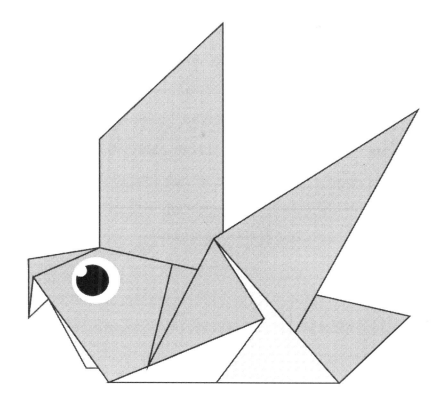

The complete pigeon

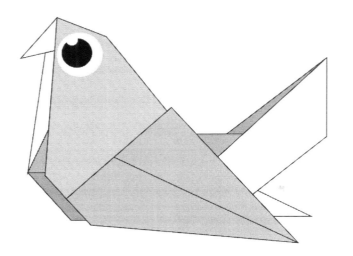

Pigeon

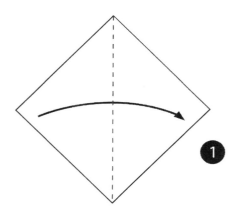

Step 1) Fold the paper in half.

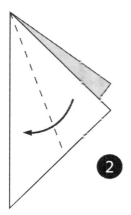

Step 2) Fold the top layer of paper over along the dotted line.

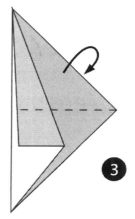

Step 3) Fold the top half of the paper in behind the model.

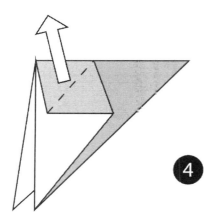

Step 4) Open up the top flap of paper and Squash Fold it flat. Take a look at the next diagram to see the final position of the paper.

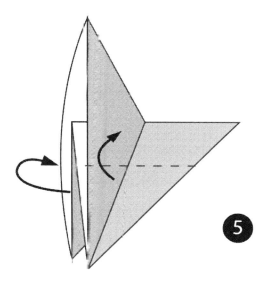

Step 5) Fold the paper up along the dotted line and repeat on the other side.

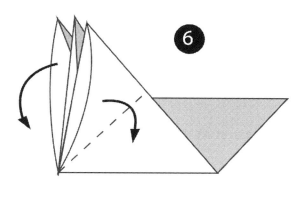

Step 6) Fold the paper down along the dotted line and repeat on the other side.

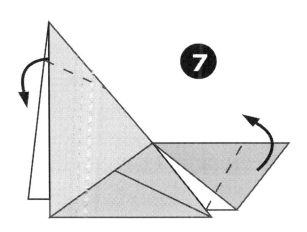

Step 7) Make an Inside Reverse Fold to form the head and make an Outside Reverse Fold to make the tail.

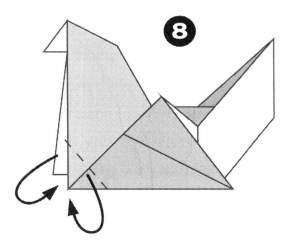

Step 8) Fold the paper inside along the dotted line and repeat on the other side.

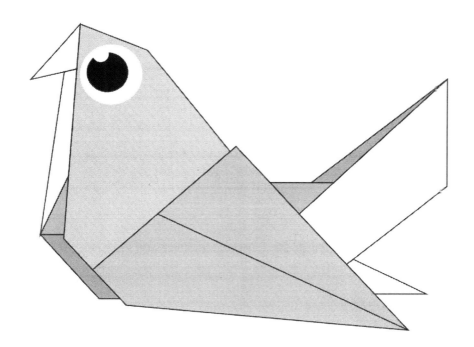

The complete pigeon

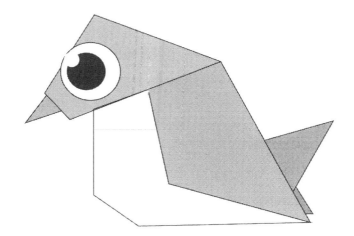

Pigeon

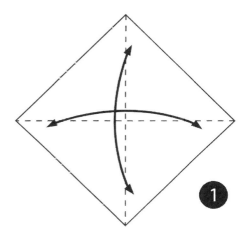

Step 1) Fold and unfold the paper in half both ways.

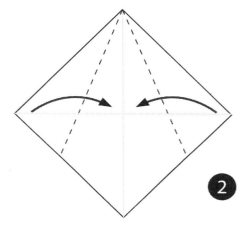

Step 2) Fold both sides in towards the centre along the dotted lines.

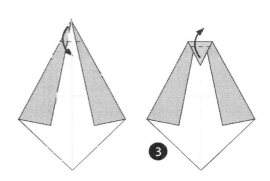

Step 3) Make a Pleat Fold at the top of the paper.

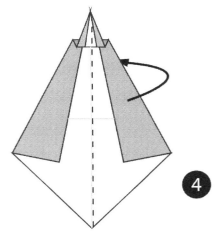

Step 4) Fold the paper in half bringing the right side behind.

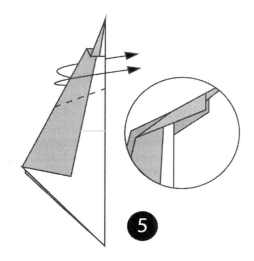

Step 5) Make an Outside Reverse Fold along the dotted line.

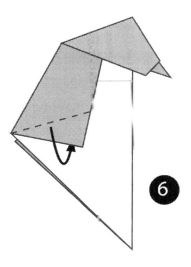

Step 6) Fold the top layer of paper underneath along the dotted line.

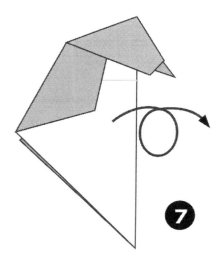

Step 7) Turn the paper over.

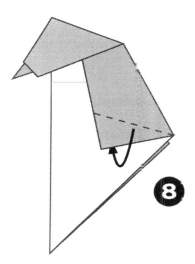

Step 8) Fold the top layer of paper underneath like on the other side.

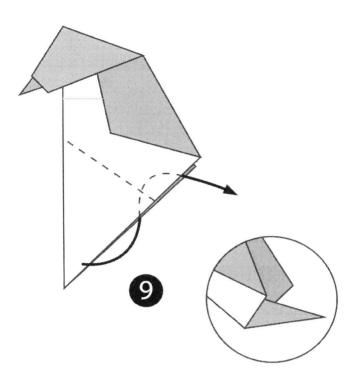

Step 9) Make an Inside Reverse Fold along the dotted line.

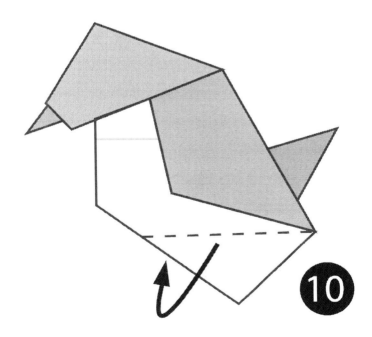

Step 10) Fold the bottom of the paper behind the model.

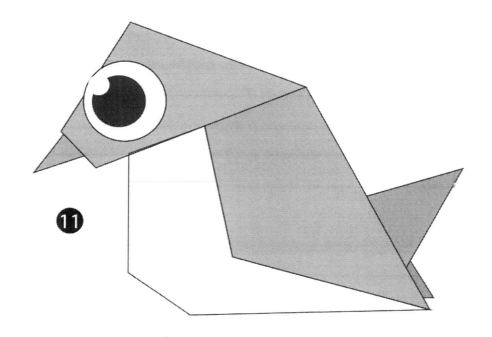

The complete pigeon

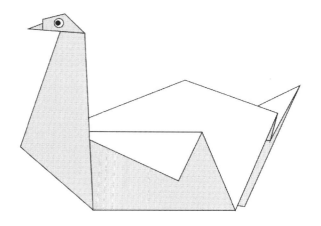

Swan

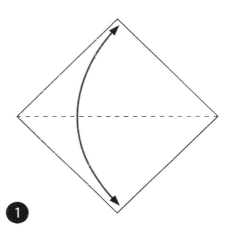

Step 1) Fold the paper in half and then unfold it.

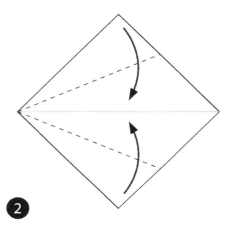

Step 2) Fold both sides in to the centre along the dotted lines.

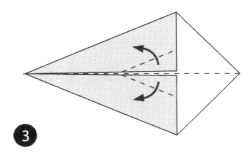

Step 3) Fold the top layers of paper out along the dotted lines.

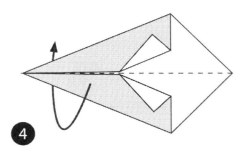

Step 4) Fold the paper in half bringing the bottom up and behind.

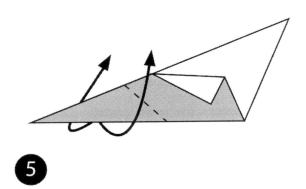

Step 5) Make an Outside Reverse Fold along the dotted line.

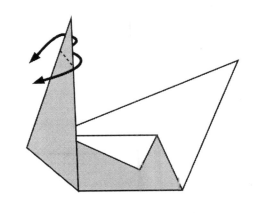

Step 6) Make another Outside Reverse Fold along the dotted lines

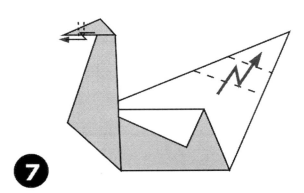

Step 7) Make a Crimp Fold on the head to form the beak and make another Crimp Fold on the back to form the tail.

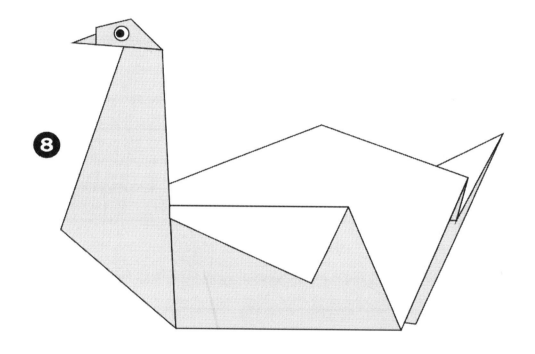

The complete swan

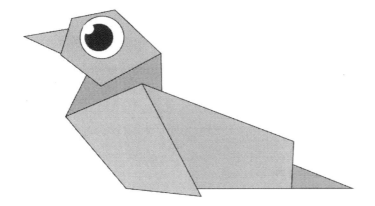

Duck

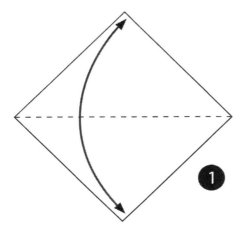

Step 1) Fold the paper in half and unfold it.

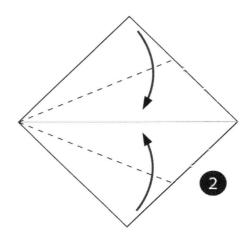

Step 2) Fold both sides of the paper to the centre along the dotted lines

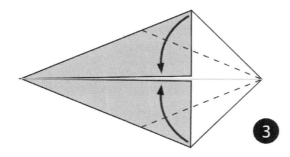

Step 3) Fold the top and bottom to the centre along the dotted lines.

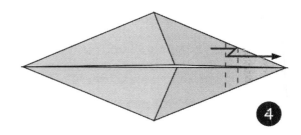

Step 4) Make a Pleat Fold along the dotted lines.

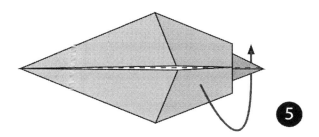

Step 5) Fold the paper in half to the back

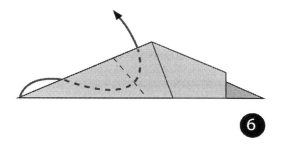

Step 6) Make an Inside Reverse Fold along the dotted line.

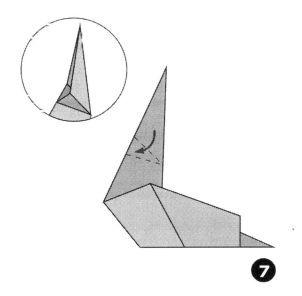

Step 7) Open up the paper along the dotted lines and Squash Fold it flat. Take a look at the next step to see the final position of this fold.

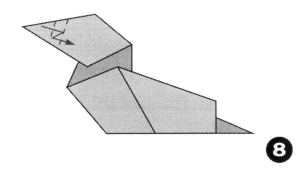

Step 8) Make a Pleat Fold behind the model to form the beak.

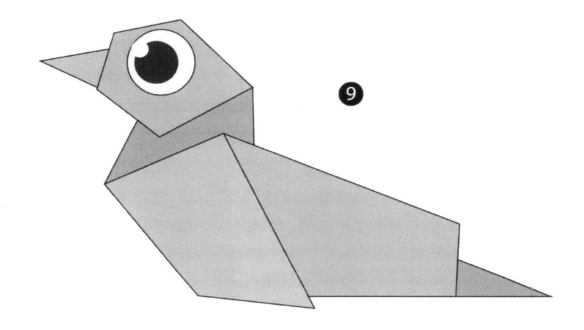

The complete duck

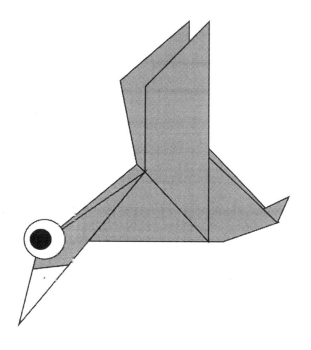

Flying duck

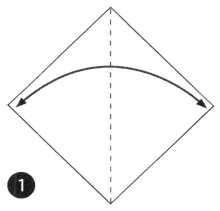

Step 1) Fold the paper in half and then unfold it.

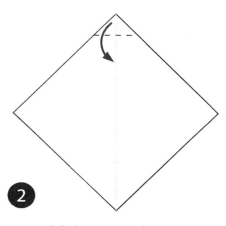

Step 2) Fold the top of the paper down along the dotted line.

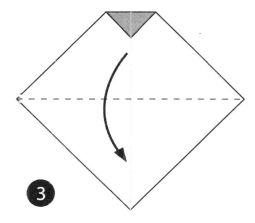

Step 3) Fold the paper in half along the dotted line.

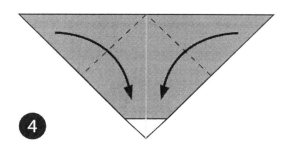

Step 4) Fold the two sides down along the dotted lines.

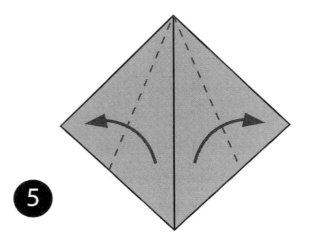

Step 5) Fold the sides out along the dotted lines.

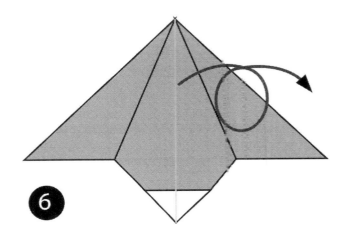

Step 6) Turn the paper over.

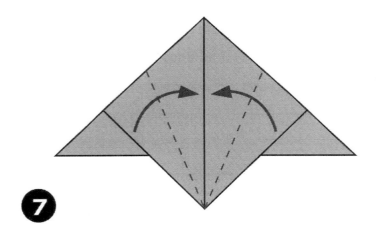

Step 7) Fold the sides in along the dotted line. Flatten the wings so they look like they do in the next step.

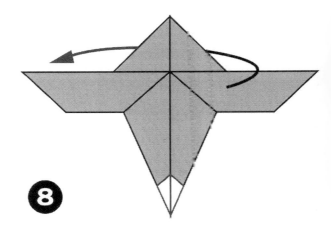

Step 8) Fold the paper in half over behind the model.

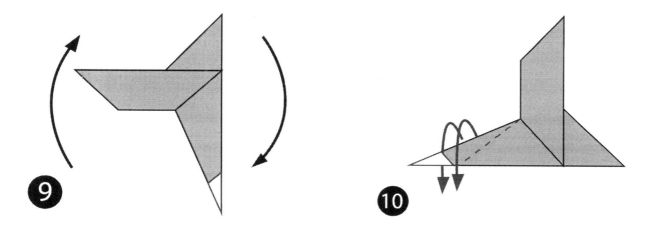

Step 9) Rotate the model about 90 degrees

Step 10) Make an Outside Reverse Fold along the dotted line.

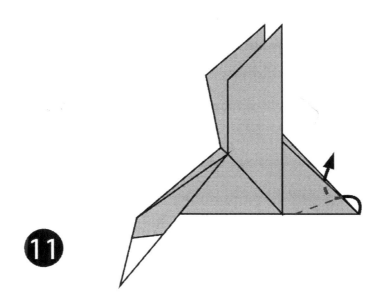

Step 11) Make an Inside Reverse Fold along the dotted line to form the tail.

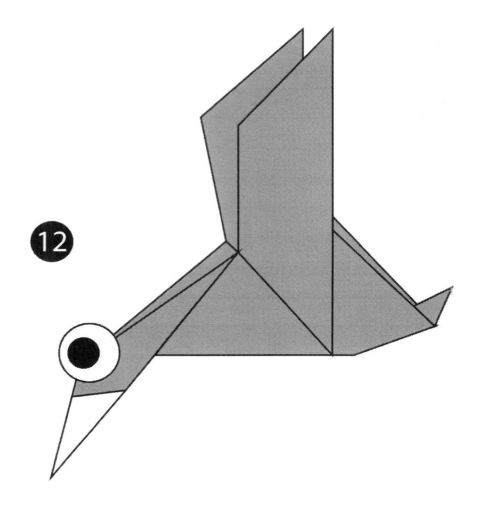

The complete flying duck

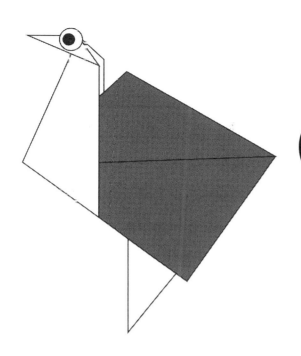

Ostrich

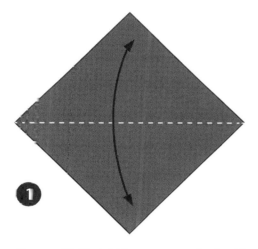

Step 1) Fold the paper in half and then unfold it.

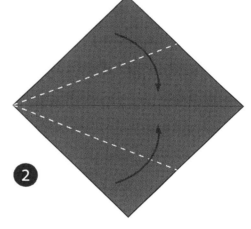

Step 2) Fold both sides in the the centre along the dotted line.

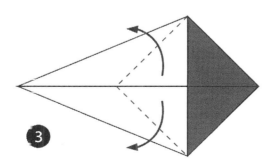

Step 3) Fold the top layers of paper out along the dotted lines.

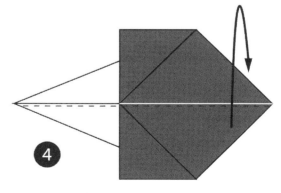

Step 4) Fold the paper in half behind the model.

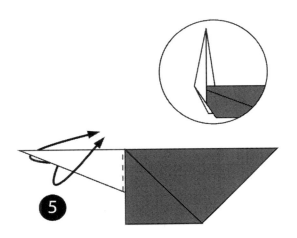

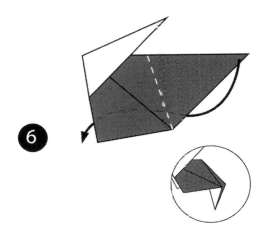

Step 5) Make an Outside Reverse Fold along the dotted line.

Step 6) Make an Inside Reverse Fold along the dotted line.

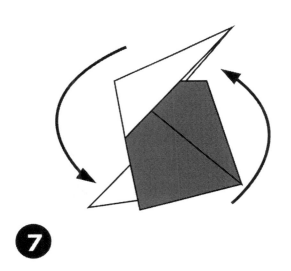

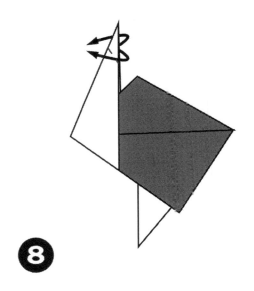

Step 7) Rotate the model about 90 degrees.

Step 8) Make an Outside Reverse Fold along the dotted line to form the head.

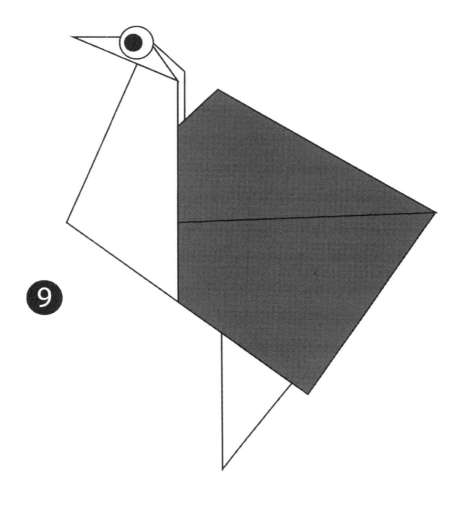

The complete ostrich

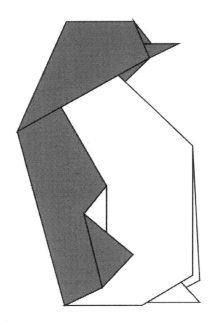

Penguin

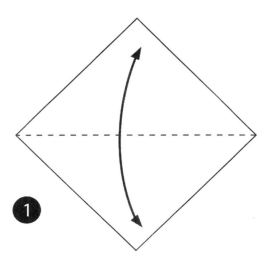

Step 1) Fold the paper in half and then unfold it.

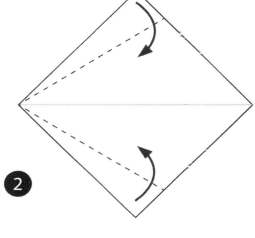

Step 2) Fold both sides in to the centre along the dotted line.

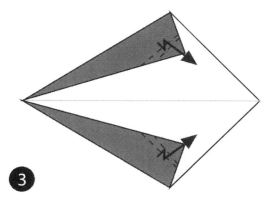

Step 3) Make two Pleat Folds along the dotted lines.

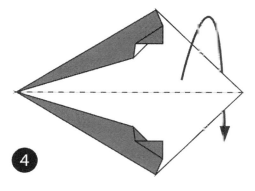

Step 4) Fold the paper in half bringing the top half behind.

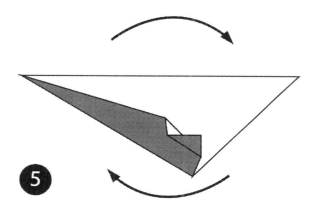

Step 5) Rotate the paper about 45 degrees.

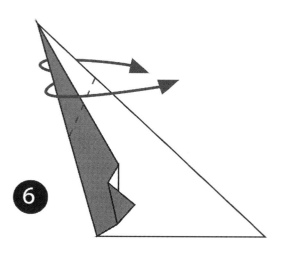

Step 6) Make an Outside Reverse Fold along the dotted lines.

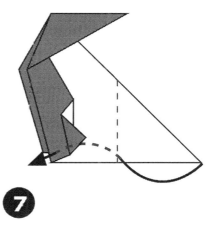

Step 7) Make an Inside Reverse Fold along the dotted line.

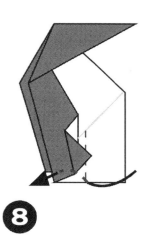

Step 8) Inside Reverse Fold the Inside Part again over to the right. The diagram shows an arrow pointing to the left but it's wrong...

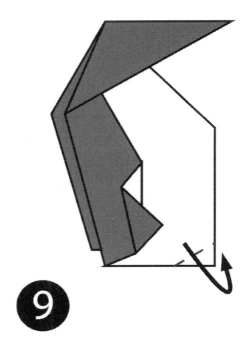

Step 9) Fold the top flap of paper underneath along the dotted line and then repeat on the other side.

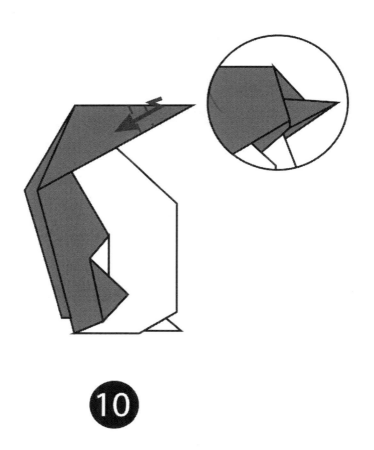

Step 10) Make a Crimp Fold along the dotted lines.

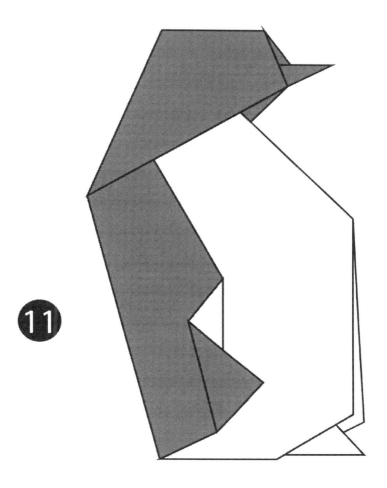

The complete penguin

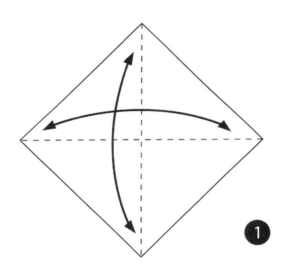

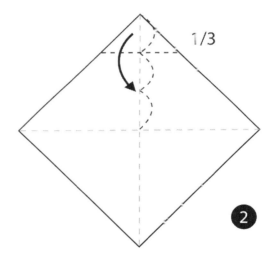

Step 1) Fold and unfold the paper in half both ways.

Step 2) Fold the top part of the paper down about a third of the way from the top to the middle.

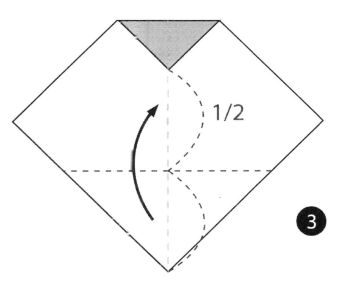
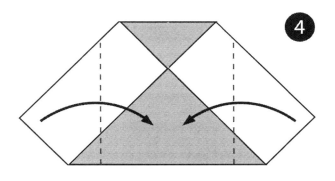

Step 3) Fold the bottom of the paper about half of the way between the bottom and the tip of the triangle at the top.

Step 4) Fold both sides in along the dotted lines.

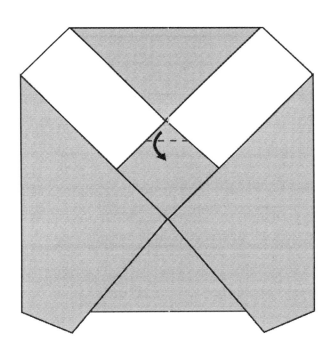

Step 5) Fold the tip of the paper down to make the beak.

The complete owl

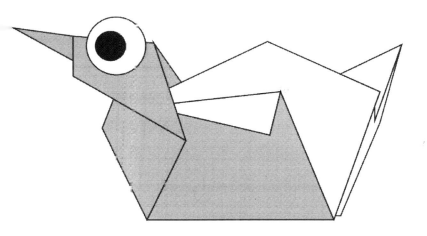

Duck

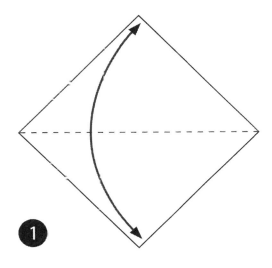

Step 1) Fold the paper in half and then unfold it.

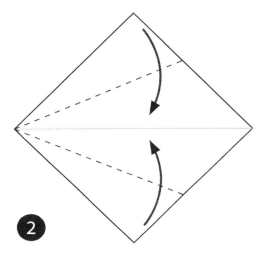

Step 2) Fold the top and bottom of the paper to the centre along the dotted lines.

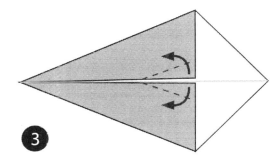

Step 3) Fold the top layers of paper out along the dotted lines.

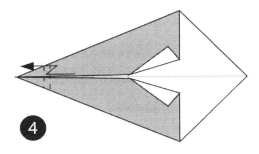

Step 4) Make a Pleat Fold along the dotted lines behind the model.

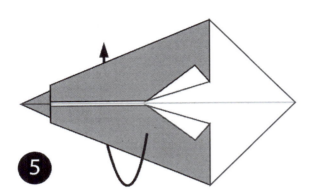

Step 5) Fold the paper in half.

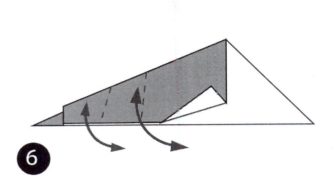

Step 6) Fold and unfold the paper along the dotted lines. You'll use these creases in a later step.

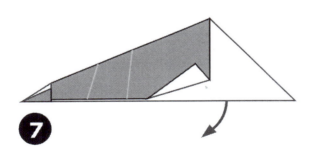

Step 7) Open the paper back up.

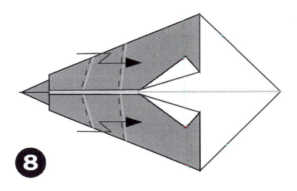

Step 8) Make a Pleat Fold using the creases from step 6.

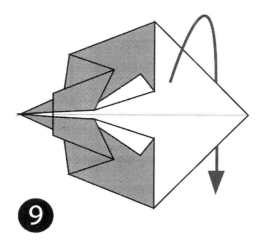

Step 9) Fold the paper in half.

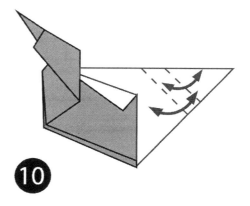

Step 10) Fold and unfold the paper along the dotted lines. You'll use these creases in a later step.

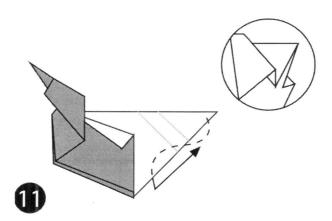

Step 11) Make a Crimp Fold using the creases from the previous step.

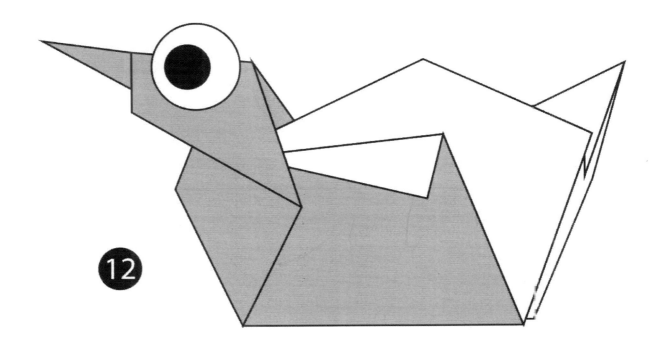

The complete duck

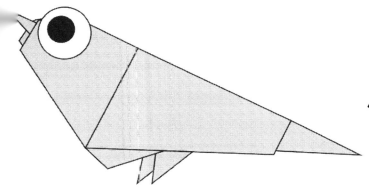

Sparrow

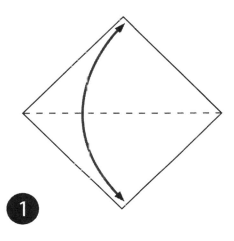

Step 1) Fold the paper in half and then unfold it.

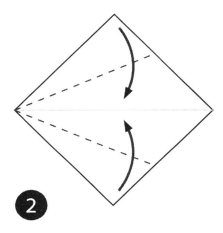

Step 2) Fold the top and bottom in to the centre along the dotted lines.

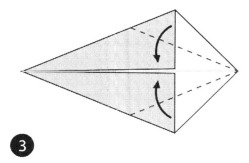

Step 3) Fold the top and bottom in to the centre along the dotted lines.

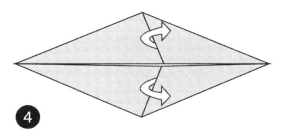

Step 4) Open up the paper trapped inside on both sides.

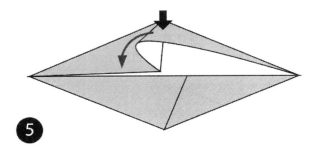

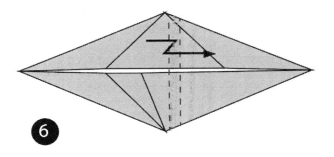

Step 5) Push the paper flat into a Rabbit Ear Fold on the top and bottom. This will result in a Fish Base.

Step 6) Make a Pleat Fold along the dotted lines.

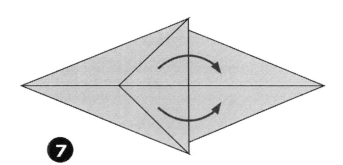

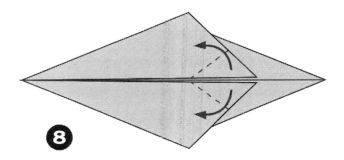

Step 7) Fold the two Rabbit Ear flaps over to the right.

Step 8) Fold the paper out along the dotted lines.

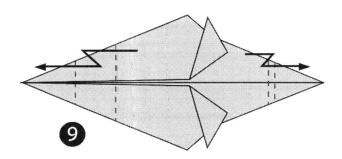

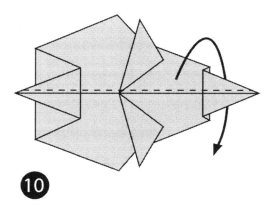

Step 9) Make a Pleat Fold on the left and on the right.

Step 10) Fold the paper in half bringing the top part down and behind.

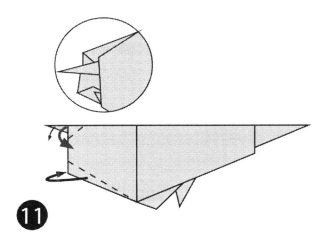

Step 11) Fold the beak down a little bit, then fold the bottom of the head underneath and repeat on the other side.

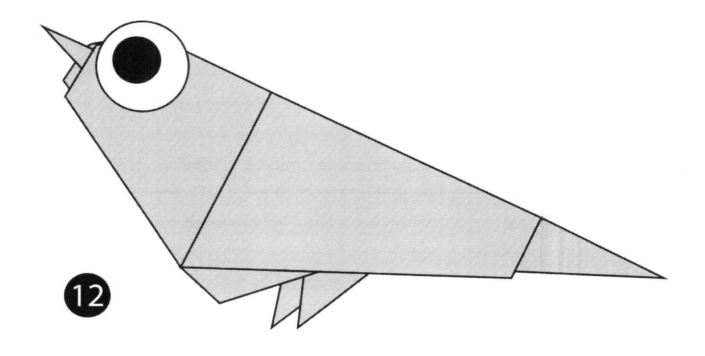

The complete sparrow

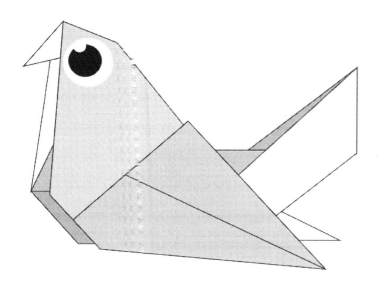

Pigeon

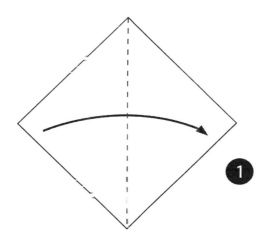

Step 1) Fold the paper in half.

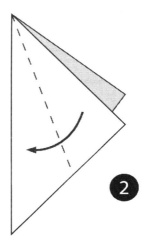

Step 2) Fold the top layer of paper over along the dotted line.

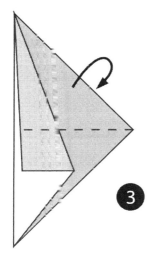

Step 3) Fold the top half of the paper in behind the model.

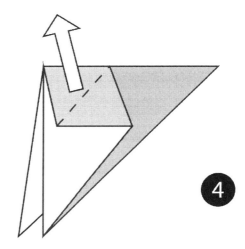

Step 4) Open up the top flap of paper and Squash Fold it flat. Take a look at the next diagram to see the final position of the paper.

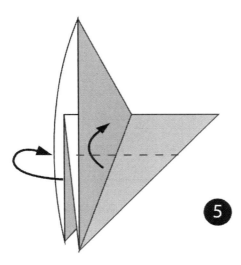

Step 5) Fold the paper up along the dotted line and repeat on the other side.

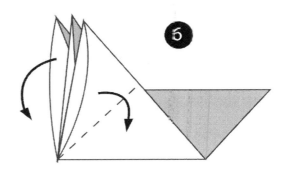

Step 6) Fold the paper down along the dotted line and repeat on the other side.

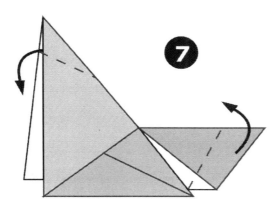

Step 7) Make an Inside Reverse Fold to form the head and make an Outside Reverse Fold to make the tail.

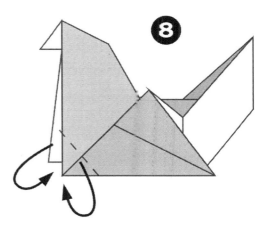

Step 8) Fold the paper inside along the dotted line and repeat on the other side.

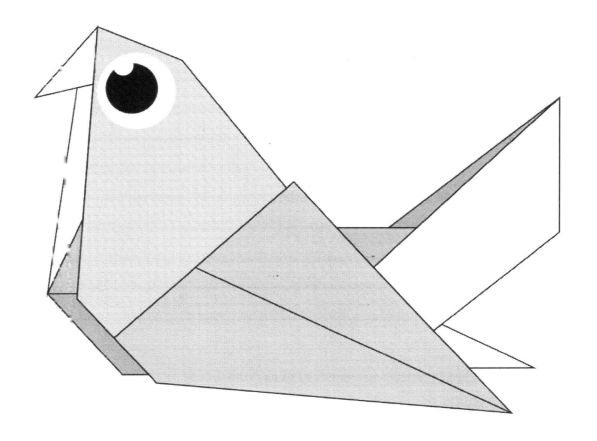

The complete pigeon

Printed in Great Britain
by Amazon